11 WAYS
— TO SHARE —
THE GOSPEL WITH DIGITAL NATIVES

MATT GUEVARA

© 2014 Awana® Clubs International

Scripture quotations are from The Holy Bible, English Standard Version® (ESV®), copyright ©2001 by Crossway, a publishing ministry of Good News Publishers. Used by permission. All rights reserved.

TABLE OF CONTENTS

1. Set Aside The Way You Learn 8
2. Embrace Technology 12
3. Make It Visual 16
4. Keep It Active 20
5. Gather A Circle 24
6. Create A Connection 28
7. Increase Variety 32
8. Become A Guide 36
9. Lean Into Discovery 40
10. Trust The Holy Spirit 44
11. Let The Learner Practice And Teach 48

WE HAVE AN EPIC STORY TO TELL.

And when it comes to the children we have the privilege of serving, the gospel, matters most. We live in a digital world and the kids growing up in this context need the gospel to be told powerfully and boldly in ways they will understand.

The challenge is for us to push the boundaries to share the gospel, capturing the heart, renewing the mind, and shaping digital learner's stories with transforming truth. It's time to be captivating, visual, compelling, and authentic as we take the unscripted, audacious risk to see a generation of technologically savvy kids swept up in God's grand narrative, changed by the Author of salvation's epic masterpiece, the redemption story penned throughout history.

I invite you to join this journey. To take this risk. To explore. To dream. To discover. To work together in sharing the Gospel with digital learners.

1
SET ASIDE THE WAY YOU LEARN

SET ASIDE THE WAY YOU LEARN

Teachers teach the way they learn. We do not drift naturally toward new learning styles; we stick closely to the contours of our learning experiences. We lecture. We expect uninterrupted silence.

Yet, today's kids are fundamentally different than you and me in the way they think, process, use, and share information. Scientists have confirmed today's kids have vastly different neurological patterns than previous generations, so much so that the developmental stages we have adopted over the last 50 years may need to be redefined.

So the task falls to the adults charged with ministering to today's kids to become learners ourselves. It esteems the learners among us when we set aside the way we learn and dive into their world. When we become students of the learners in our ministries, we open up ourselves to a deep connection with those we are called to reach with the gospel.

What are you learning about the kids in your context? Have you read anything recently to help you understand their digital world? The remaining pages in this book are dedicated to helping you understand digital learners and share the gospel with them.

2
EMBRACE TECHNOLOGY

EMBRACE TECHNOLOGY

Nostalgia is like a grammar lesson: You find the present tense and the past perfect.
– *Owens Lee Pomeroy*

Remember the Fischer-Price® Record Player or the View Master®? Remember board games and Lincoln Logs®? The Rubix's® Cube and Tiddly Winks? I'm sure these toys bring back fine memories of days gone by; days we sometimes wish to reclaim.

Those days are gone.

And at some point in history, the tools that replaced free time for previous generations became a feared enemy of the church. Media and technology in children's ministry has largely been criticized as entertainment and fluff. Yet media and technology are profoundly important tools in the teaching and learning process and it's time for children's ministry to fully embrace these tools, not vilify them. From Children's Television Workshop to the Khan Academy® to the App Store, options abound alongside access. Children's Technology Review reveals "more products have been published in the past 48 months than in the first 27 years of children's interactive media." A simple search in the iTunes™ app store reveals thousands of apps tagged for kids.

Try asking some kids in your ministry what apps they are playing or what websites they are using and think of a way to apply it to your ministry.

To help you get started, try VoiceThread®, Canva®, Slidebean, or Toontastic.

3
MAKE IT VISUAL

MAKE IT VISUAL

I never liked doing geometry.

Correction, I never liked and continue to actively dislike geometry. But I'll never forget watching Bill Cosby teach geometry on public television with his marker and magic drawing board. What was so fascinating about Bill Cosby teaching geometry with his magic drawing board?

It was visual (and the sound effects were amazing).

Today's kids prefer to process sound, color, and video before text. So often in children's ministry we lead with text and add visual elements later. But the learners among us need to see it to learn it. So find pictures and icons to help you share the gospel. Look at Little Visuals, Unsplash, The Pattern Library, and the Public Domain Archive.

Draw your own visuals. You might be reading this right now with the firm conviction that you do not know how to draw. Can you write every number from 1 to 9 and every letter from A to Z, both upper and lower case? Guess what? You know how to draw.

Pictures are far more powerful than words to the kids in your ministry, so make the gospel visual whenever you share it.

4 KEEP IT ACT

KEEP IT ACTIVE

How many times have you said the phrase "crisscross applesauce"?

If it's more than five times, please wash your mouth out with heavy whipping cream.

Crisscross Applesauce can create confusion in a children's ministry. First, why applesauce? I can think of far better rhymes for crisscross. What about "Like a boss?" Second, it tends to be the most repeated message a leader gives to the kids. That message translates, "I need you to sit still and be quiet."

Here's the reality: more than 60 percent of students today are visual-kinesthetic learners. What they see and put into practice, they learn. Yet many times, children's ministry leaders still stand in front of a group of kids lecturing for long periods of time. All the activity, if any, comes at the beginning of the ministry hour. Think about this: how much time do you devote in children's ministry to asking kids to sit and listen, crisscross applesauce like a boss? Can you change that pattern to fit the natural way kids respond to the gospel?

When you share the gospel, move around. Get kids moving. Give students a chance to follow the verbs you use with actions of their own. Put away the script, skip the monologue, and move a little.

5
GATHER A CIRCLE

so excited for #Awana tonight!

2 min ago via facebook for iphone comment like

me too! I'll see you there!
5

I heard there is a theme night tonight?

silly socks! bring yours :)
14

glad I saw this...almost forgot!!!
8

Finally, an excuse to wear these ;)
2

GATHER A CIRCLE

Social networking has been woven into the fabric of nearly every culture.

In 2014, 80 percent of Facebook's nearly 1.3 billion users are outside North America. Facebook® is available in 70 languages and users have the ability to assist in the development of new translations. Twitter® has 255 million monthly active users and most of them are using the service on a mobile device outside the United States.

Facebook. Twitter. Snapchat®. Instagram™. These tools are native to the digital learner. And because today's kids have grown up with these tools at their fingertips, it has given digital kids an appetite to learn collaboratively. Digital learners desire to network simultaneously with others.

This preference has a shadow side. Spend time with one of today's technologically savvy kids and you might discover that while they may interact effortlessly with a screen, they may not respond as well face-to-face. They need your help, not only to share the gospel but to share the gospel relationally. Leaders need to model and offer deep friendships so the gospel can be seen and lived out within the life of the faith community.

6
CREATE A CONNECTION

CREATE A CONNECTION

**Do one thing,
Do it very well,
And then do the next.**
 - Origin unknown

My father repeated this phrase to my siblings and me more times than I can remember. Focused attention and grit are the fuel required to get things done, right? However, digital learners prefer multitasking and parallel processing over focus. It's why they can do their homework on a laptop while watching TV carrying on a conversation via text with a friend — and still be bored.

A 2006 Kaiser Foundation report written by Victoria Rideout and Elizabeth Hamel titled "The Media Family: Electronic Media in the Lives of Infants, Toddlers, Preschoolers, School Age Children and Their Parents," revealed that a week in the life of an average school-age child includes half an hour with Dad, 2.6 hours with Mom, 2.2 hours doing homework, half an hour reading for pleasure, and more than 25 hours — near the equivalent of a full-time job or a week of school — watching television, playing video games, and interacting with digital devices. Today's kids are completely comfortable with the visual bombardment of simultaneous images, text, and sounds because, for them, such experiences provide relevant and compelling experiences that can convey more information in a few seconds than can be communicated by reading an entire book.

As you share the gospel, create connections. Do not be afraid to multitask. Tell the story while you are building something. Give them ideas about where to find out more about the history and background online.

7
INCREASE VARIETY

INCREASE VARIETY

In a video game, there is a great synergy between structure and freedom.

The structure is simple: you need to save the princess and in order to do that you need to sail to the castle, in order to sail you need a boat, in order to build a boat you need wood, to get wood you need an ax, that dwarf over there has an ax so go get him. It is up to the player to defeat the dwarf and overcome each obstacle.

It is within this world of structure and freedom that digital learners thrive. However, we often bypass variety in our ministry contexts because we want more structure, not less. We often circumvent freedom in Christian education settings because we are more concerned with keeping things developmentally appropriate.

The challenge for you and me is to ruthlessly attack the issue of monotony as we share the gospel. Could you write down your Sunday schedule for the age group you work with from memory? If you can do it, so can the digital learners in your ministry.

Where can you increase variety in your ministry setting? What elements can you switch, alter, hack, eliminate, elongate, flip, or bedazzle so the students in your ministry have no idea what is coming next?

8 BECOME A GUIDE

BECOME A GUIDE

Digital learners are different than previous generations of kids and they require a new kind of leader to share the Gospel with them.

Gever Tulley, a master teacher of digital learners and creator of the Tinkering School gives a new perspective on the traditional teacher role: "Adults are collaborators, not teachers, present to guide an exploration, not teach through a series of goals." In Tulley's explanation of an activity for kids involving motors and batteries, he offers this directive: "Adult collaborators need to wait 10 minutes before nudging the kids in the right direction." Think about that — 10 minutes!

That may be the length of time we have for the ENTIRE gospel presentation! So many times in our ministries, we will not wait 10 seconds before telling our groups the right answer or redirecting them.

In traditional learning environments, the teacher knows everything and dispenses knowledge to the group slowly. We could benefit from changing the role of small group leader to guide and partner, not the ultimate source of all knowledge. Instead of giving detailed instructions, give one guiding question and hand over the tools.

Instead of closed questions (how many times did Jesus ask Peter, "Do you love Me?"), increase the number of open questions (what would you say if Jesus asked you about your love?).

9 LEAN INTO DISCOVERY

LEAN INTO DISCOVERY

We are perishing for want of wonder, not for want of wonders. – *G.K. Chesterton*

I love the response I get when I show my kids new things. Like how maifun rice sticks change in hot oil. There's something amazing that happens when we discover things we never knew before. Discovery inspires wonder and awe. Wonder and awe motivate more discovery.

Discovery is a powerful learning tool. It invites expanded curiosity. But so often, as we do children's ministry and share the gospel we focus more on getting the right information to the child than on the learner discovering God's truth. Telling rips discovery out of the learning process and replaces it with memorization.

We've based so much of our children's ministry programming on information download instead of Holy Spirit upload. What we've found is that if a child has been in church long enough, they are one of the good kids who know everything. But we've blinded their faith with facts. The challenge is to step away from the information and allow children to experience faith, to empower digital learners to express what God is doing in their lives, to let them wrestle with hard truths and tough teaching, and to unleash their creativity with open-ended questions and apps and tools and freedom.

10

TRUST THE HOLY SPIRIT

TRUST THE HOLY SPIRIT

OK, I know this may have been hard for to read so far. Take heart and do not be discouraged. I recognize that many of the ways I suggest you share the gospel with digital learners are new and may look different to you. Let me encourage you to trust the Holy Spirit.

I love John 16, where Jesus promises the Holy Spirit to His followers. His followers are reaching a turning point in their relationship with Jesus. It's likely that they're wondering 'what's next' and in need of some encouragement. Knowing their hearts and their deepest needs, Jesus makes them a phenomenal promise.

He says: I still have many things to say to you, but you cannot bear them now. When the Spirit of truth comes, He will guide you into all the truth, for He will not speak on His own authority, but whatever He hears He will speak, and He will declare to you the things that are to come (John 16:12-13).

As you share the gospel, do so in the boldness and power that comes from the Holy Spirit living inside you. You know the gospel; now share it confidently with the children in your ministry, recognizing that it is God who does the work of drawing kids to His Son Jesus.

11
LET THE LEARNER PRACTICE & TEACH

LET THE LEARNER
PRACTICE & TEACH

Jay Rosen correctly identifies this generation as *"the people formerly known as the audience."*

This generation no longer wants just to be the audience; they want to be the actors. They expect, want, and need interactive information, interactive resources, interactive communications, and relevant, real-life experiences.

What the research tells us is that on average after two weeks we recall:

- Less than 10 percent of the content we read
- About 20 percent of what we hear, like from a lecture
- 20 to 30 percent of content processed simultaneously using two or more media, like looking at pictures or watching a movie
- About 30 percent of lessons involving demonstration

- About 50 percent of content that we hear and see while watching a demonstration that uses two or more media simultaneously
- 65-80 percent of content that involves practice like participating in a discussion or giving a talk
- About 90 percent that involves the teaching of a concept to others as well as the immediate application of the learning within the context of a real time, real world task or a simulation of that task

As you share the gospel, give the digital learners you are trying to reach a chance to respond by sharing the gospel with others.

MATT GUEVARA

A veteran #kidmin, Matt holds a deep curiosity for how kids learn and his innovative views on the new horizon of ministry in the digital world have earned him invitations to design solutions for an array of leaders and organizations. Matt currently serves as the Executive Director of International Network of Children's Ministry and leads a family with three amazing kids.

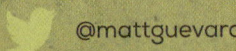 @mattguevara   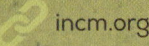 incm.org